pitch fuckin black

A good pitch

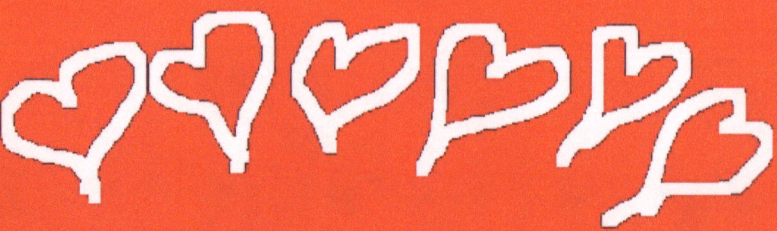

now here is the dream we
ll speak every three years
and when i m in love with
someone else
u ll unstuck me

A gun

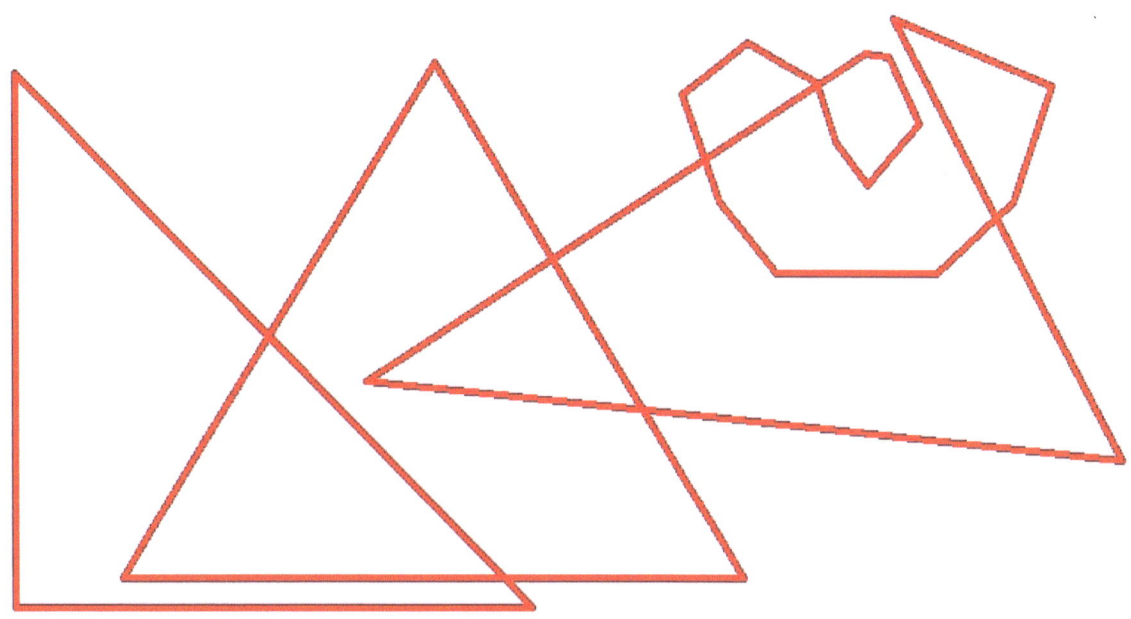

Beatin urself up hatts off

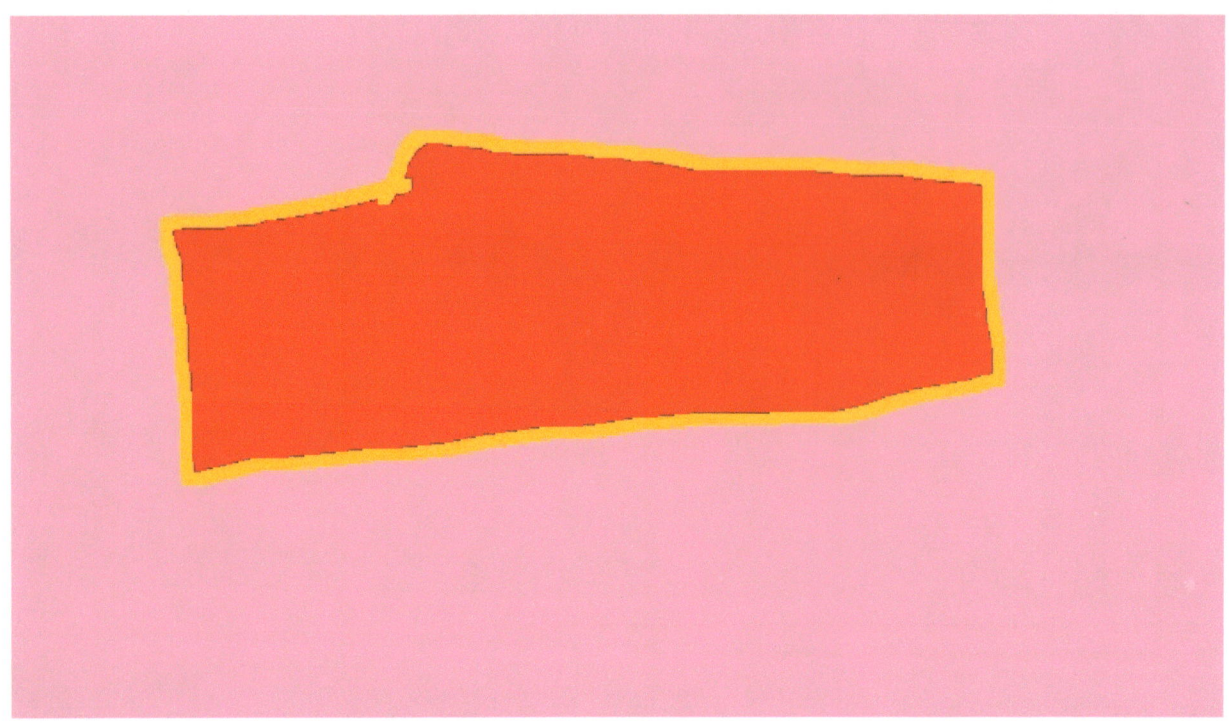

Crete

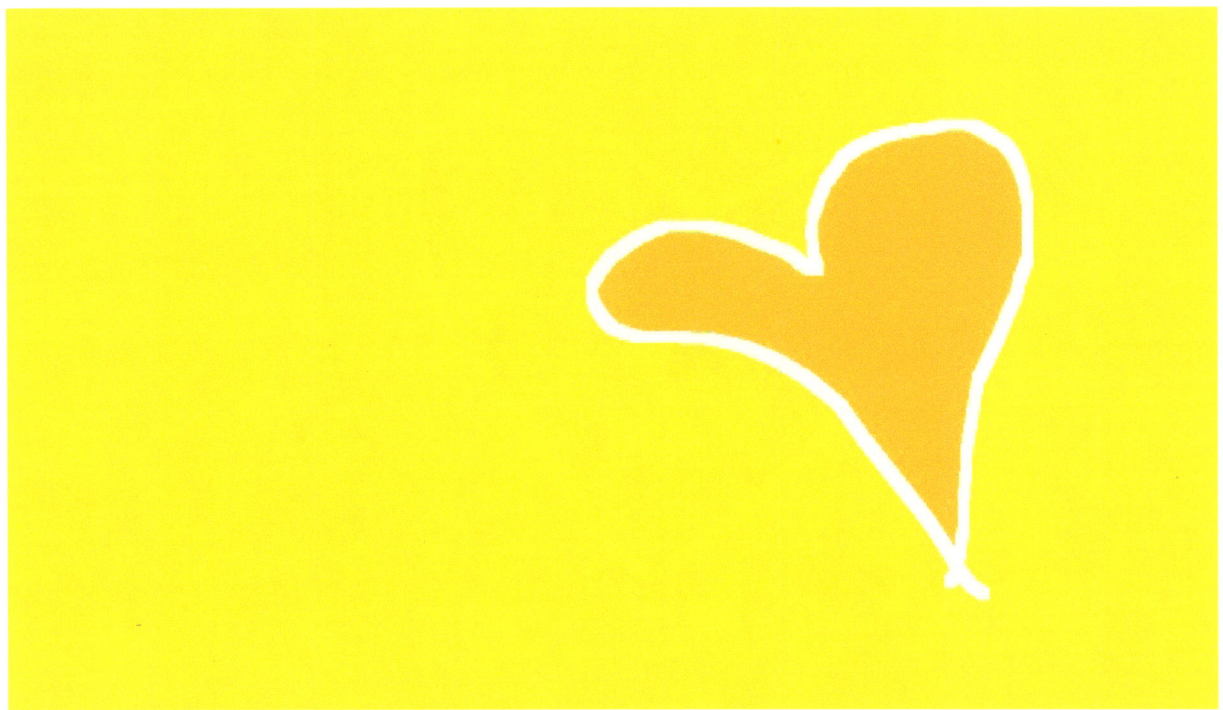

Do I exist within without the boundaries

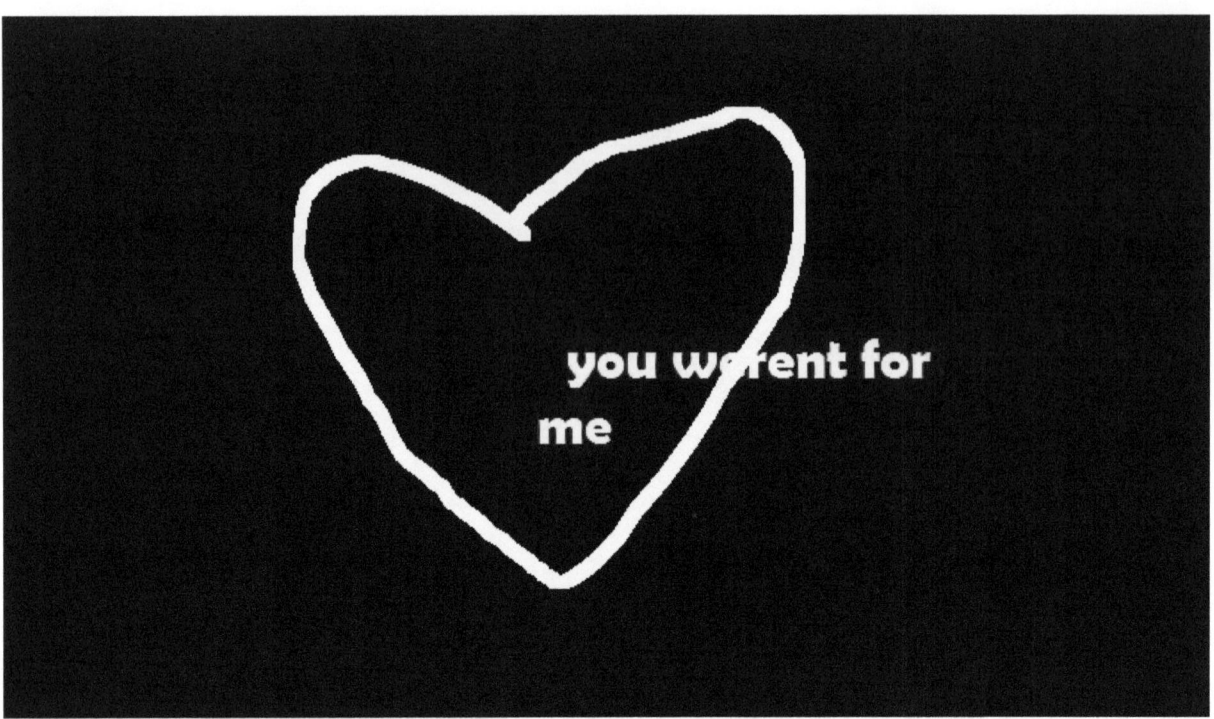

Fuck you edinbrah

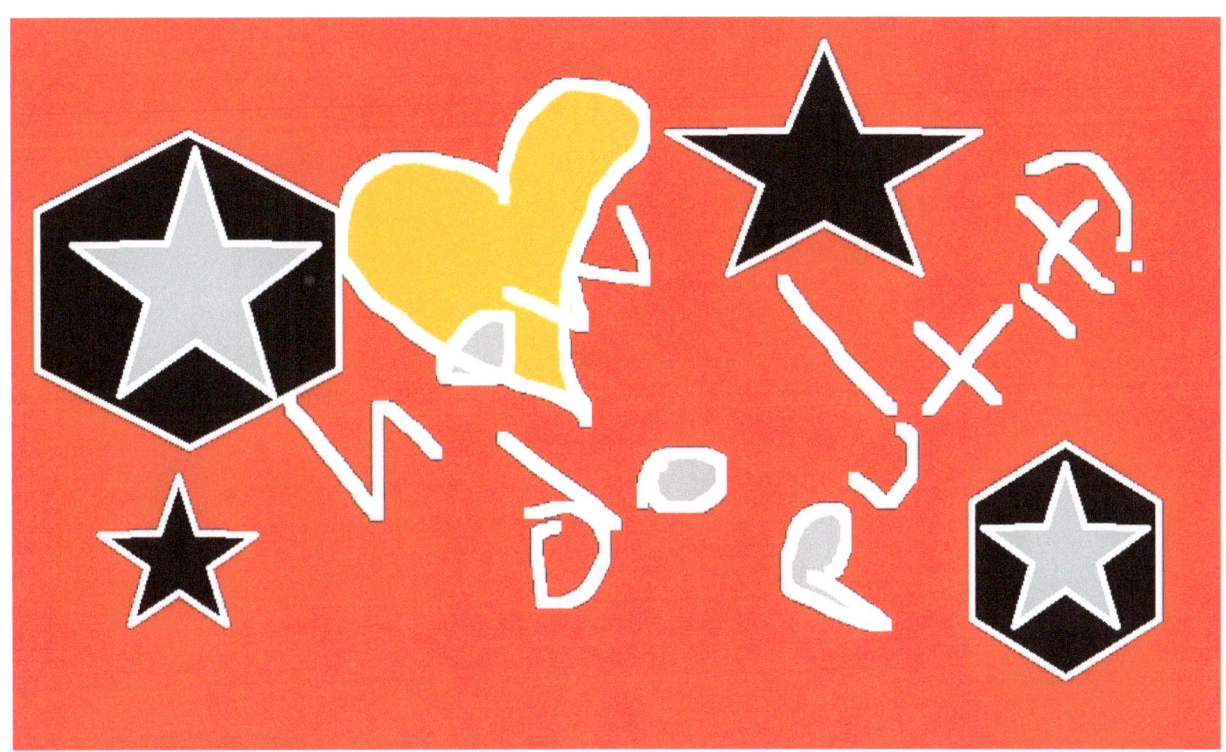

Fuckin xmas

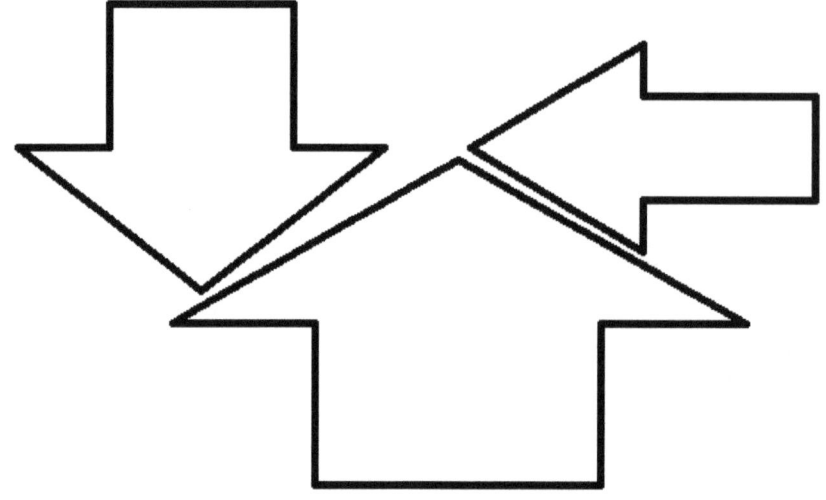

germans

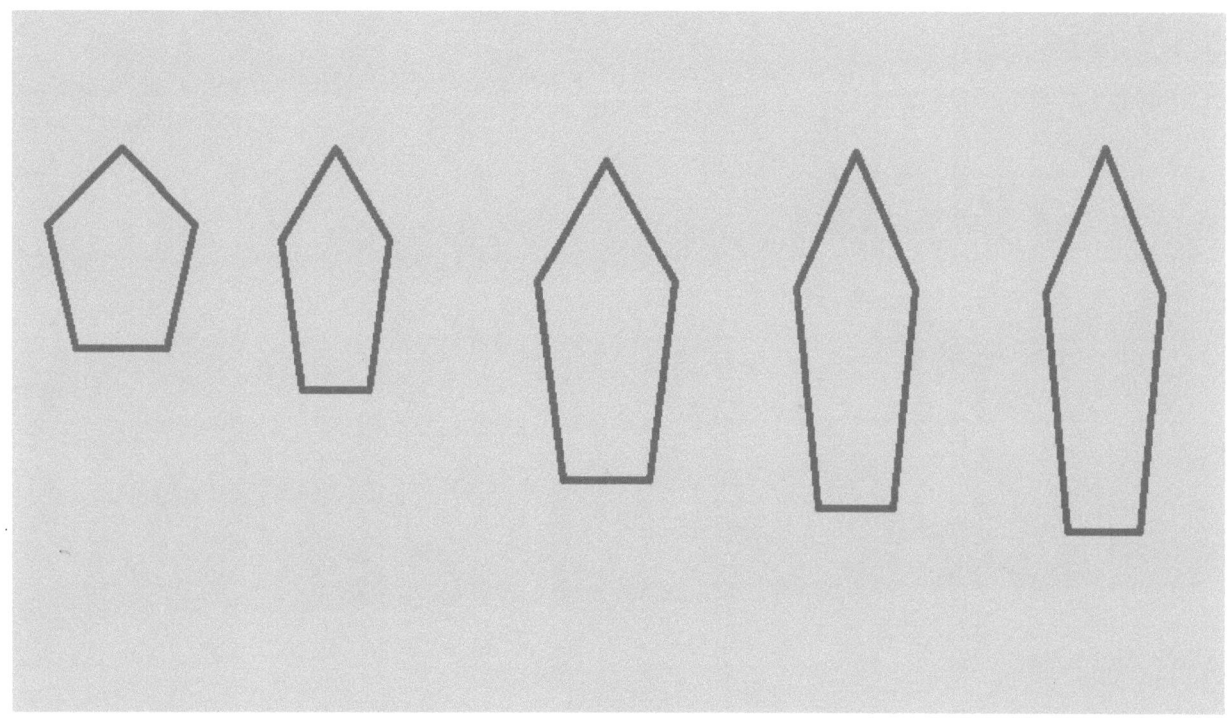

Grey or greyt

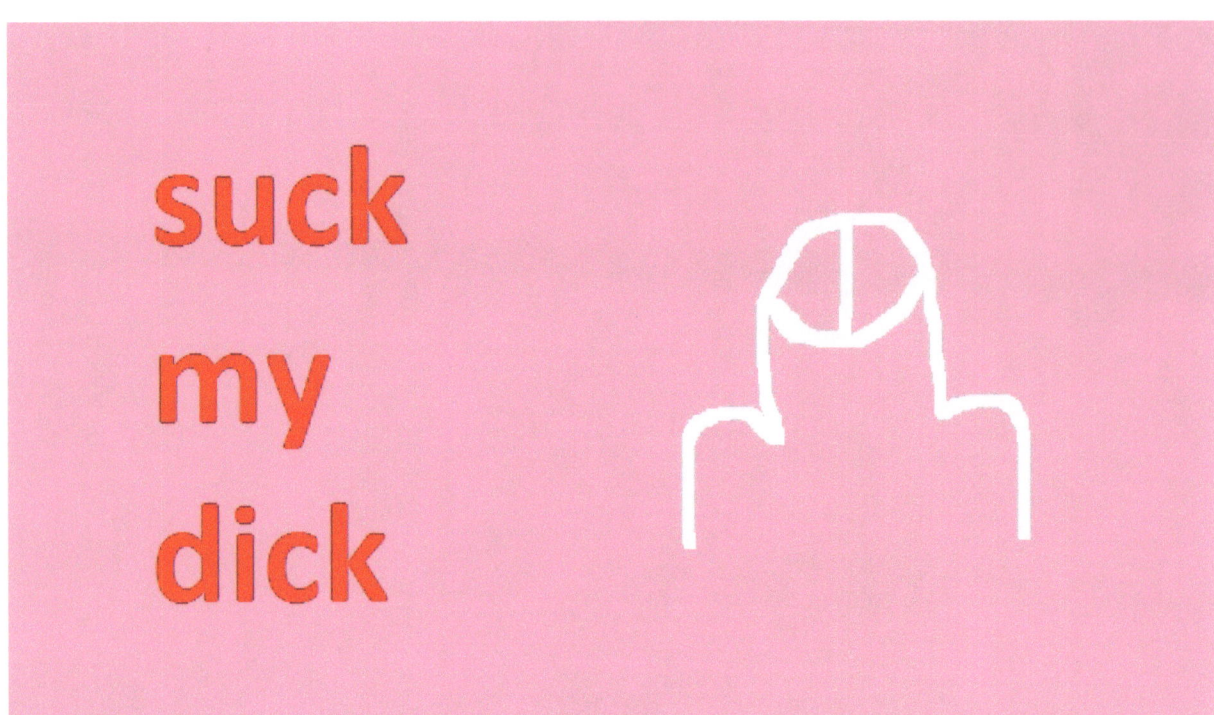

Happy anniversary

if you were allowed to kill an
ex - and it was pc- would u
hve
a done it
b regreted by now
u dont think like that
c like a cunt
or is it

I dont know paint

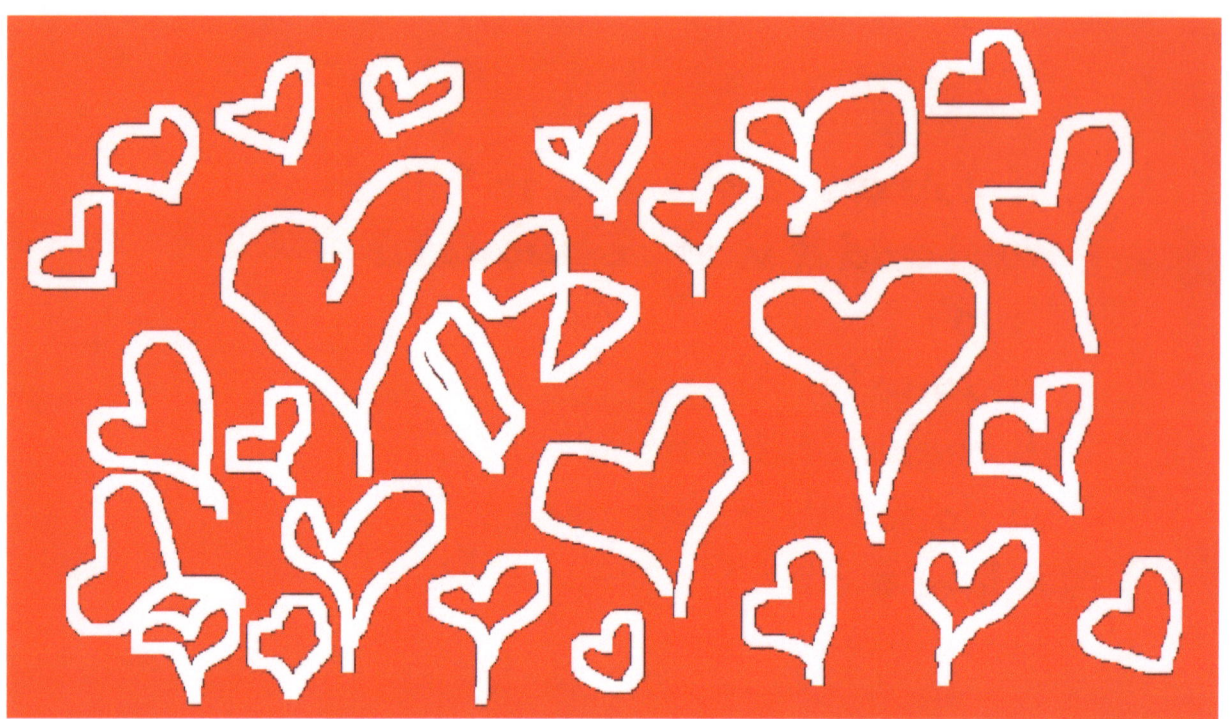

If you were

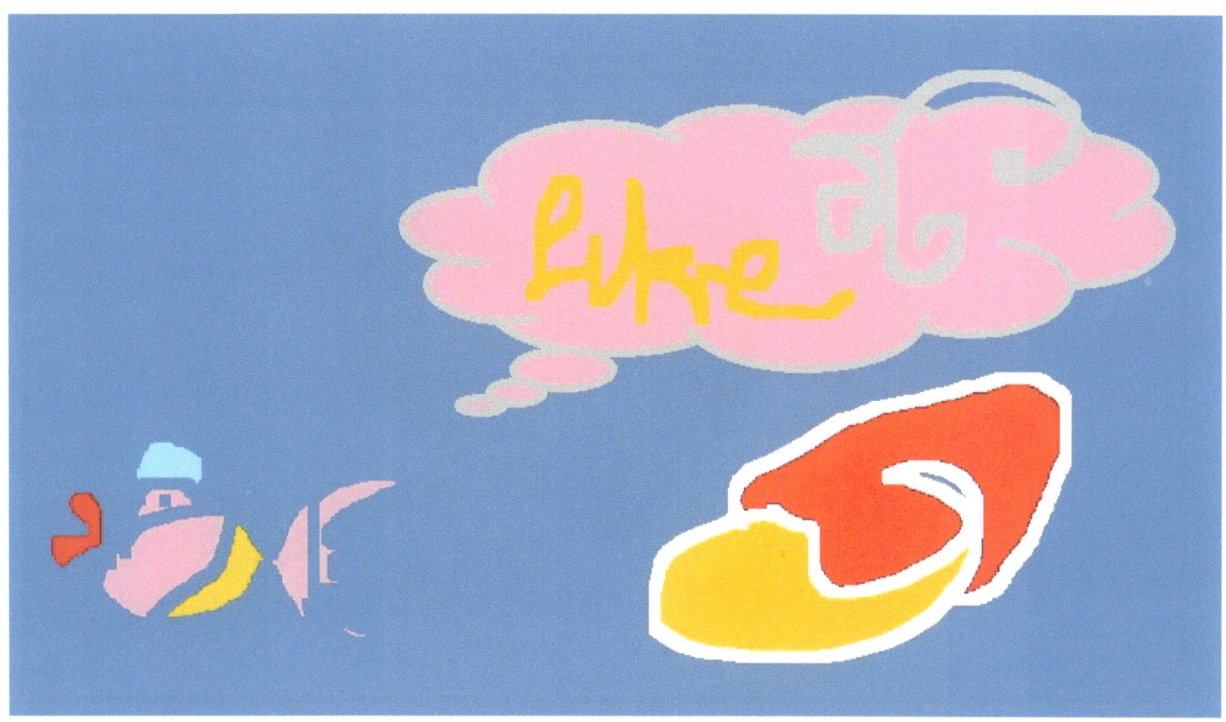

Like a f a a r t

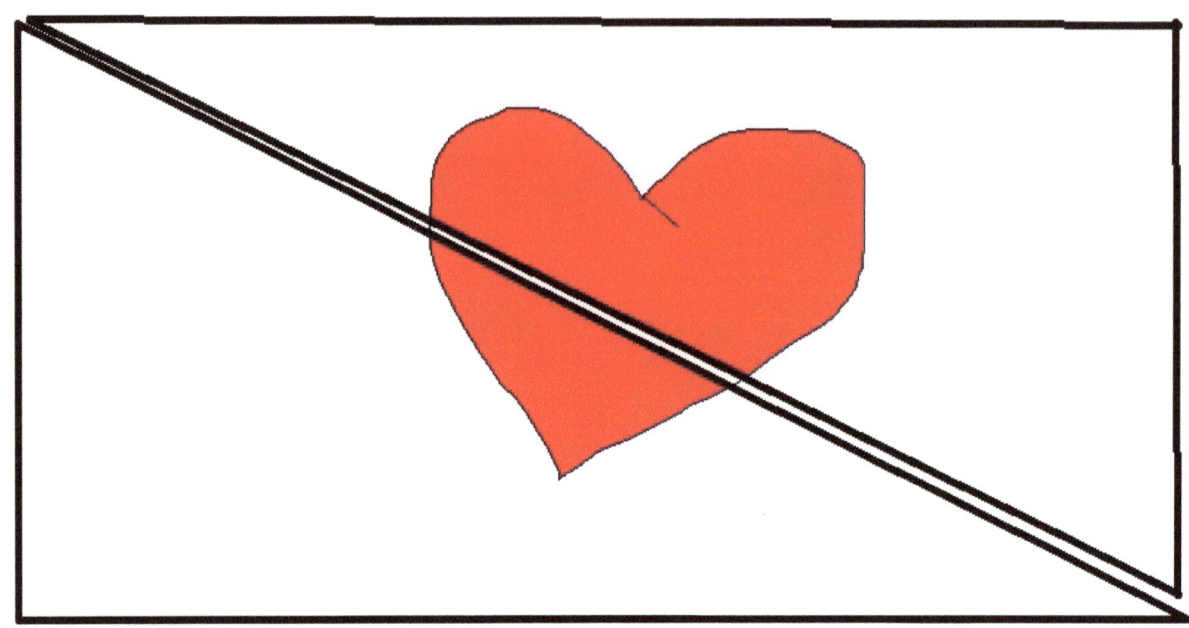

Like nothing happened

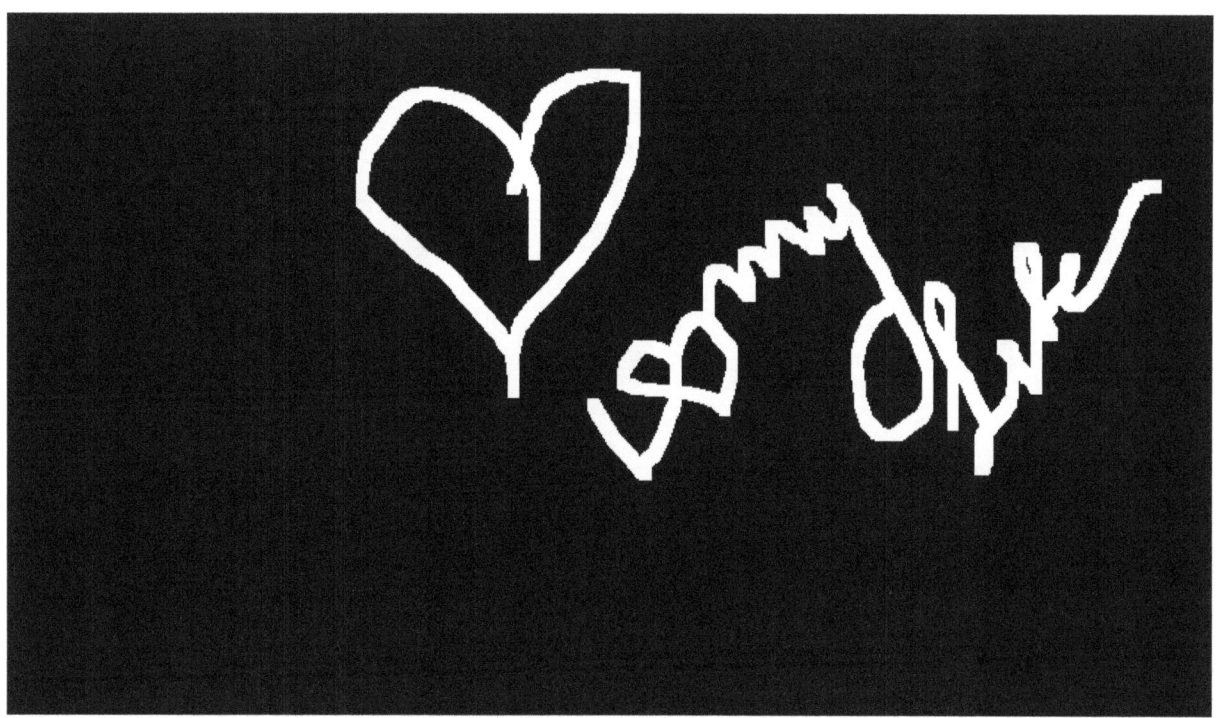

My love life

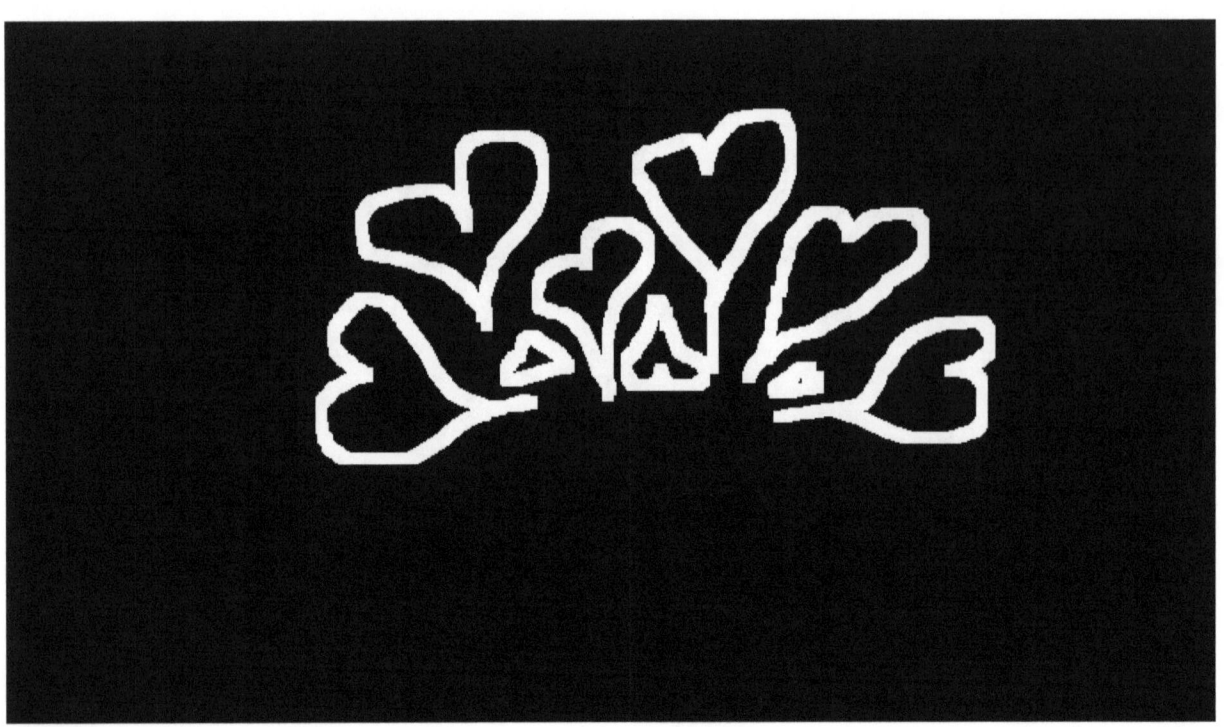
Pagoni

paint pink

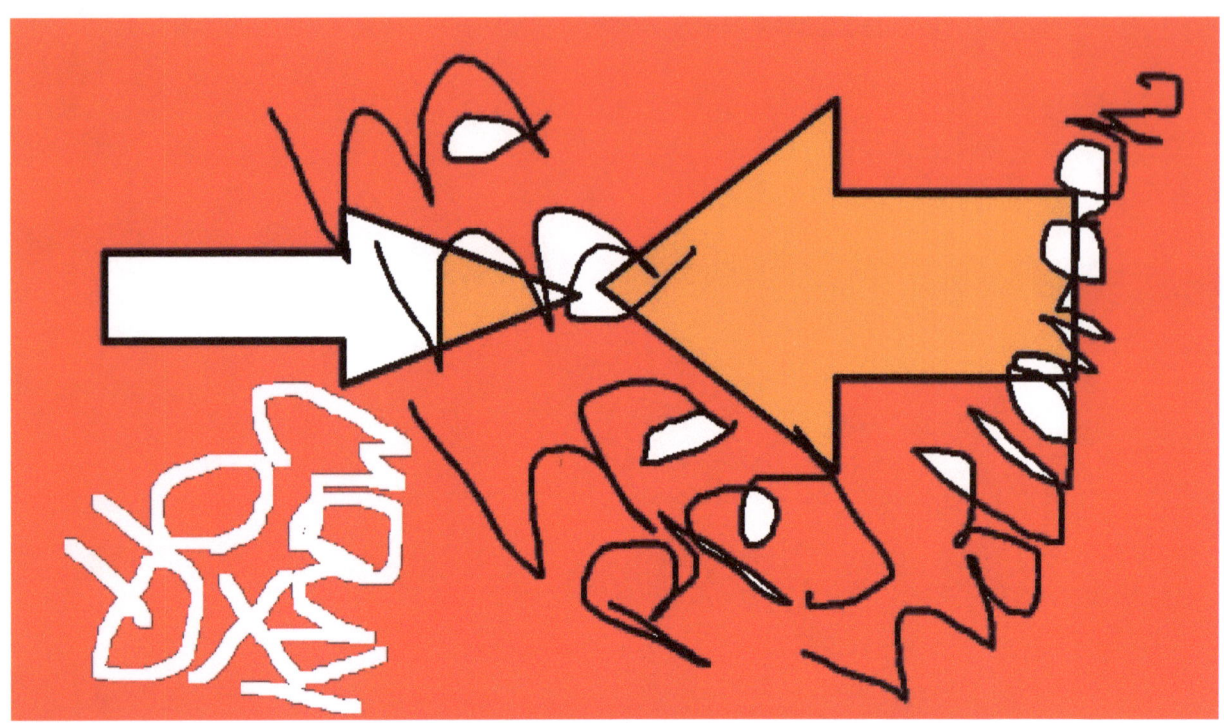

Save my ass

Smells like shit   it

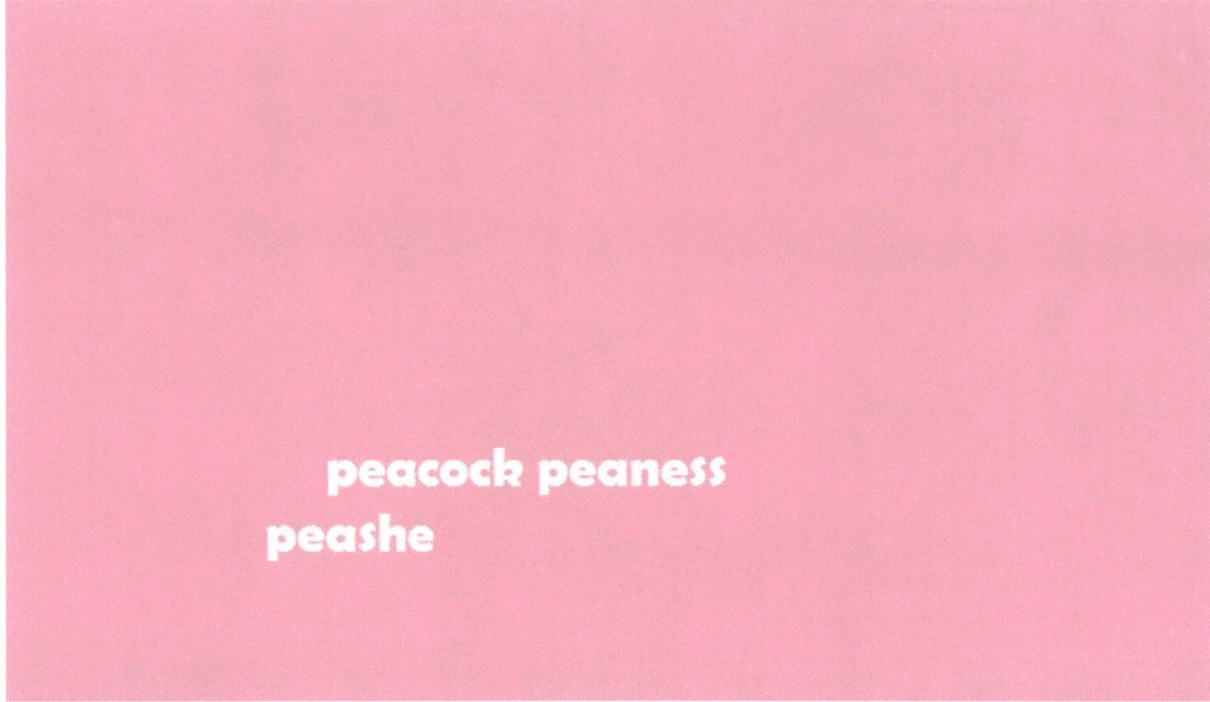

Somethin like that

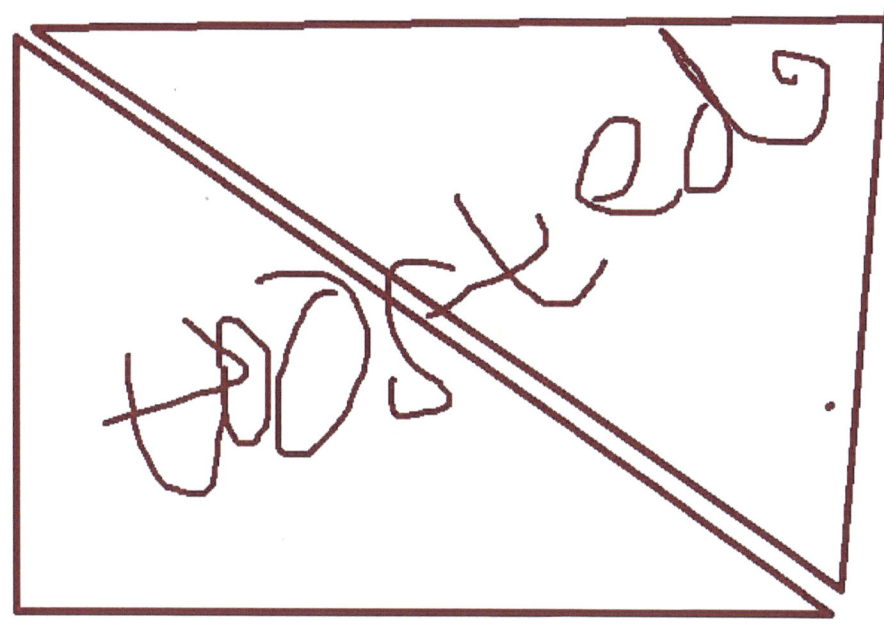

toasted

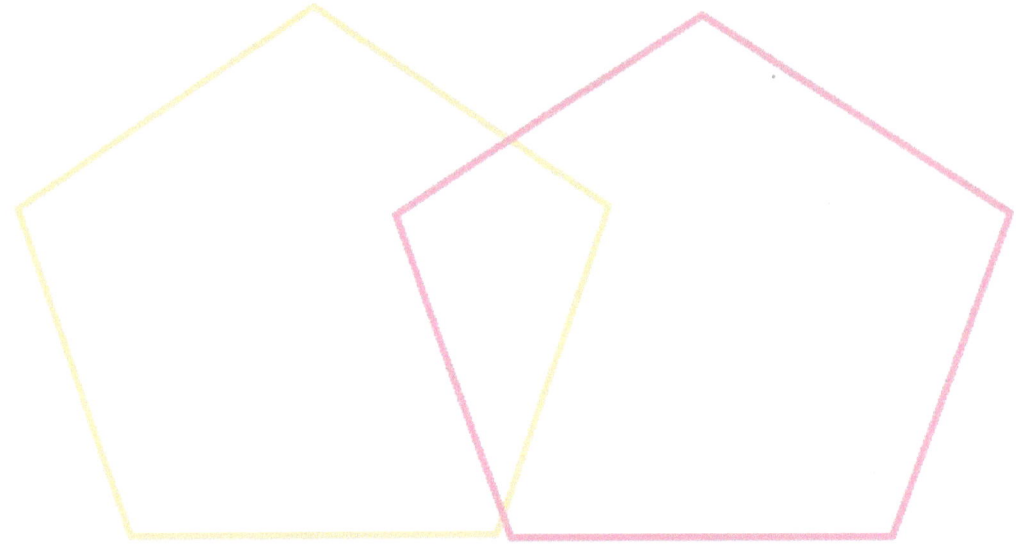

Unfinished I liked how u knew stuff

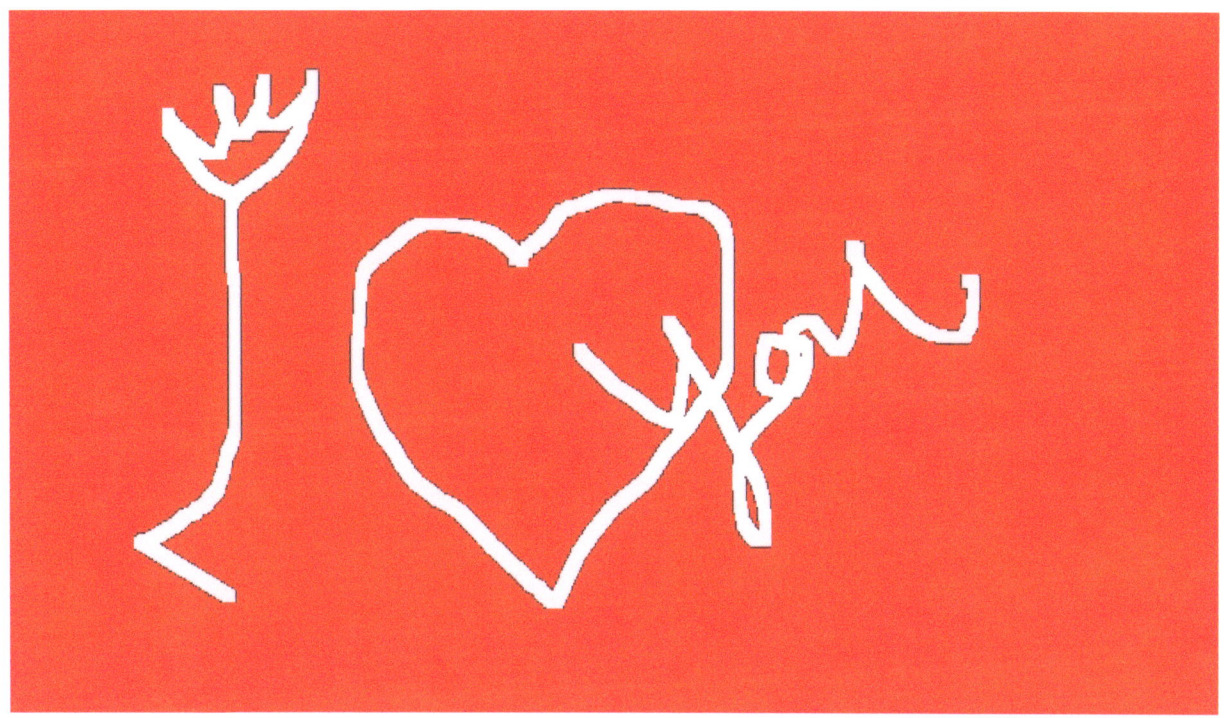

Xronia polla manula mu xx

To contact the artist email   thickandtastyxxx@gmail.com

www.ingramcontent.com/pod-product-compliance
Lightning Source LLC
Chambersburg PA
CBHW051839210526
45473CB00005B/1938